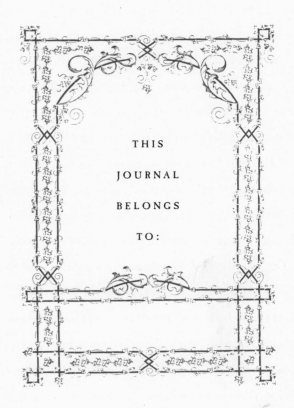

THIS

JOURNAL

BELONGS

TO:

HOW TO USE THIS JOURNAL

If you are only beginning to discover the pleasures of wildlife observation, looking at birds is perhaps an ideal way to start. There are roughly 8,800—10,200 known species of birds on the planet, making them the most varied class of terrestrial vertebrates in the world. Of these species, over seven hundred pass through North America, and roughly thirty of them regularly stop at bird feeders. These statistics illustrate the allure of bird-watching. You may start out by getting to know the manageable variety of birds in your backyard, but the undeniable thrill of seeing and identifying other members of this diverse class makes further exploration almost inevitable. You may travel in pursuit of birds but in the process gain access to the wonderful diversity of the natural world: the plant life, the terrain, and the seasons.

This journal is divided into three primary sections: Field Notes, Sketches and Photographs, and the Life List. For those who are actively in pursuit of new birds, the species checklist in the back of this journal serves as a treasured keepsake of this lifelong endeavor. But the thrill of the new is only a small aspect of birding; the Field Notes section of the journal is designed to encourage birders to use all of their senses in the field and to jot down observations about even the most familiar birds, such as their habitats, songs, and life rhythms. One of the best exercises in bird identification is attempting to draw birds and their distinguishing features. For obvious reasons, it is easier—but still very worthwhile—to sketch birds from field guide illustrations rather than from life. If you do happen to capture a bird on camera or paper, use the Sketches and Photographs section of the journal to document these often fleeting sightings.

This journal is designed to serve as a practical tool in the field, but it will represent so much more by the time you complete it. Your entries will serve as a collection of memories, knowledge, and wisdom gained by looking at birds.

Enjoy!

FAVORITE LOCAL BIRDS

Birds that inhabit or routinely pass through my region and the times of
year when I see them

_____

_____

_____

_____

_____

_____

_____

_____

_____

_____

_____

_____

_____

_____

_____

_____

_____

_____

_____

_____

_____

The redwing and song sparrow are singing, and
a flock of tree sparrows is pleasantly warbling.
. . . suddenly, in some fortunate moment,
the voice of eternal wisdom reaches me,
even in the strain of a sparrow, and
liberates me, whets and clarifies my
senses, makes me a competent witness.

—HENRY DAVID THOREAU

WISH LIST

Birds that I'm currently on the look-out for and birding distinctions that I would love to explore

_____

_____

_____

_____

_____

_____

_____

_____

_____

_____

_____

_____

_____

_____

_____

_____

_____

_____

Birding Supplies

- Binoculars and/or scope

- Field guides: birds, trees, wildflowers, butterflies

- Journal

- Pencils, ballpoint pen, eraser

- Shoulder bag or backpack

- Water and snacks

- Bug spray

- Sunscreen and hat

- Bird feeder (for winter watching)

- Code of Birding Ethics (supplied by the American Birding Association, americanbirding.org)

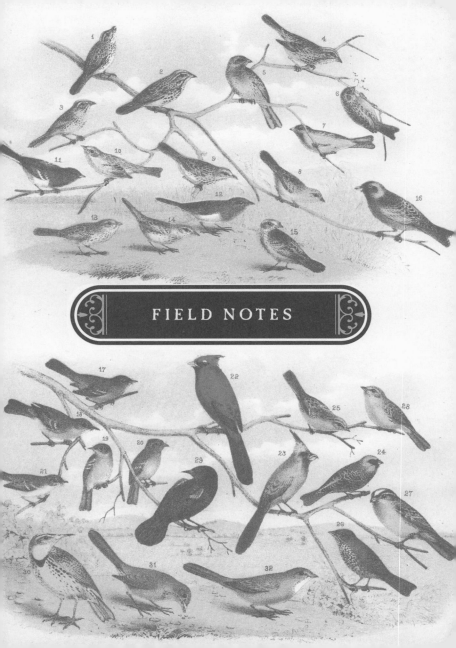

FIELD NOTES

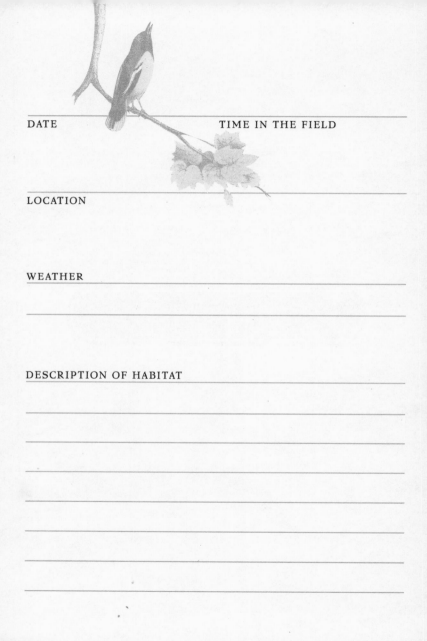

DATE _____ TIME IN THE FIELD _____

LOCATION _____

WEATHER _____

DESCRIPTION OF HABITAT _____

Species Observed

BIRDSONG DESCRIPTIONS

_____

_____

_____

_____

FIELD NOTES

_____

_____

_____

_____

_____

_____

_____

_____

_____

_____

_____

_____

_____

DATE   TIME IN THE FIELD

LOCATION

WEATHER

DESCRIPTION OF HABITAT

Species Observed

BIRDSONG DESCRIPTIONS

_____

_____

_____

_____

FIELD NOTES

_____

_____

_____

_____

_____

_____

_____

_____

_____

_____

_____

_____

_____

_____

DATE _____ TIME IN THE FIELD _____

LOCATION _____

WEATHER _____

_____

DESCRIPTION OF HABITAT _____

_____

_____

_____

_____

_____

_____

_____

Species Observed

BIRDSONG DESCRIPTIONS

_____

_____

_____

_____

FIELD NOTES

_____

_____

_____

_____

_____

_____

_____

_____

_____

_____

_____

_____

_____

DATE   TIME IN THE FIELD

LOCATION

WEATHER

DESCRIPTION OF HABITAT

Species Observed

_____   _____
_____   _____
_____   _____
_____   _____
_____   _____
_____   _____
_____   _____
_____   _____
_____   _____
_____   _____
_____   _____
_____   _____
_____   _____
_____   _____
_____   _____
_____   _____
_____   _____
_____   _____
_____   _____

BIRDSONG DESCRIPTIONS

_____

_____

_____

_____

FIELD NOTES

_____

_____

_____

_____

_____

_____

_____

_____

_____

_____

_____

_____

_____

_____

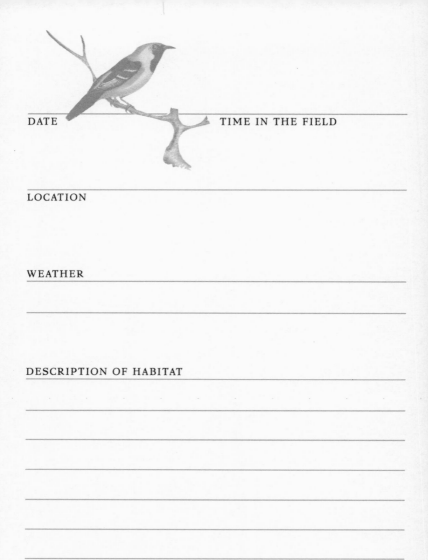

DATE _____ TIME IN THE FIELD _____

LOCATION _____

WEATHER _____

_____

DESCRIPTION OF HABITAT _____

_____

_____

_____

_____

_____

_____

_____

Species Observed

_____   _____

_____   _____

_____   _____

_____   _____

_____   _____

_____   _____

_____   _____

_____   _____

_____   _____

_____   _____

_____   _____

_____   _____

_____   _____

_____   _____

_____   _____

_____   _____

_____   _____

_____   _____

BIRDSONG DESCRIPTIONS

_____

_____

_____

_____

FIELD NOTES

_____

_____

_____

_____

_____

_____

_____

_____

_____

_____

_____

_____

_____

_____

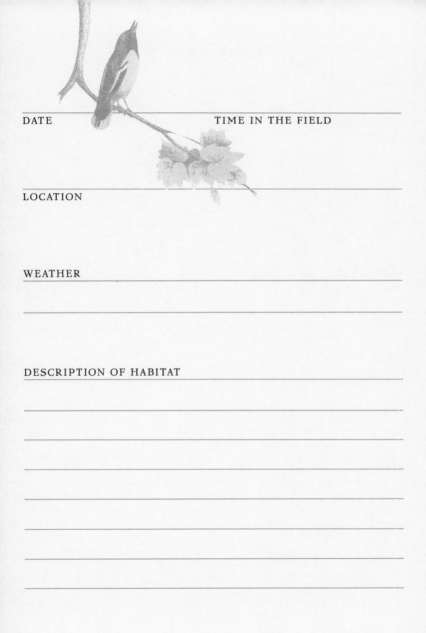

DATE   TIME IN THE FIELD

LOCATION

WEATHER

DESCRIPTION OF HABITAT

Species Observed

_____   _____
_____   _____
_____   _____
_____   _____
_____   _____
_____   _____
_____   _____
_____   _____
_____   _____
_____   _____
_____   _____
_____   _____
_____   _____
_____   _____
_____   _____
_____   _____
_____   _____
_____   _____
_____   _____

BIRDSONG DESCRIPTIONS

_____

_____

_____

_____

FIELD NOTES

_____

_____

_____

_____

_____

_____

_____

_____

_____

_____

_____

_____

_____

_____

_____

DATE _____ TIME IN THE FIELD _____

LOCATION _____

WEATHER _____

_____

DESCRIPTION OF HABITAT _____

_____

_____

_____

_____

_____

_____

_____

Species Observed

BIRDSONG DESCRIPTIONS

_____

_____

_____

_____

FIELD NOTES

_____

_____

_____

_____

_____

_____

_____

_____

_____

_____

_____

_____

_____

_____

FLOCKING TOGETHER

- Although the majority of birds are monogamous during the breeding season, about 2 percent of all birds are polygamous (the male mates with more than one female) and 1 percent polyandrous (the female mates with more than one male). Most monogamous species pair exclusively for just one season, but some species, such as pigeons, geese, and red-crowned cranes, may pair for extended periods of time or even for life.

- The gray partridge has the largest average clutch size (the total number of eggs incubated at one time), with fifteen to nineteen eggs. The albatross has the smallest clutch size, with one egg laid every two years.

- In North America, the mourning dove produces the largest amount of broods per year, raising up to six. The zebra finch, however, produces the most in the world with up to twenty-one broods a year.

- Female cowbirds refuse to build their own nests, incubate their own eggs, and raise their own young. Instead, they remove the eggs of other birds in other nests and replace the eggs with their own. Around 144 different bird species have been known to raise baby cowbirds in their own nests.

DATE _____ TIME IN THE FIELD _____

LOCATION _____

WEATHER _____

_____

DESCRIPTION OF HABITAT _____

_____

_____

_____

_____

_____

_____

_____

Species Observed

BIRDSONG DESCRIPTIONS

_____

_____

_____

_____

FIELD NOTES

_____

_____

_____

_____

_____

_____

_____

_____

_____

_____

_____

_____

_____

DATE   TIME IN THE FIELD

LOCATION

WEATHER

DESCRIPTION OF HABITAT

Species Observed

BIRDSONG DESCRIPTIONS

_____

_____

_____

_____

FIELD NOTES

_____

_____

_____

_____

_____

_____

_____

_____

_____

_____

_____

_____

_____

_____

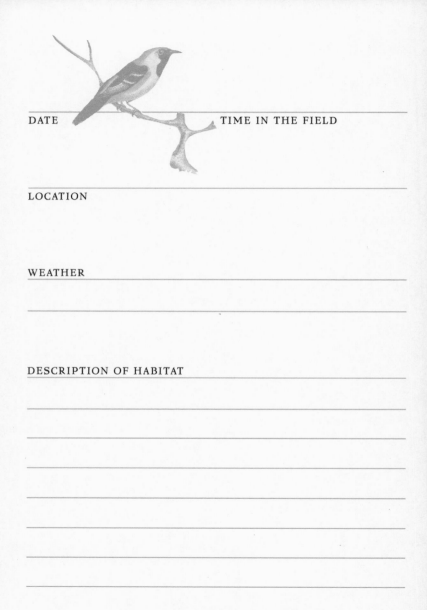

DATE _____ TIME IN THE FIELD _____

LOCATION _____

WEATHER _____

_____

DESCRIPTION OF HABITAT _____

_____

_____

_____

_____

_____

_____

_____

Species Observed

BIRDSONG DESCRIPTIONS

_____

_____

_____

_____

FIELD NOTES

_____

_____

_____

_____

_____

_____

_____

_____

_____

_____

_____

_____

_____

_____

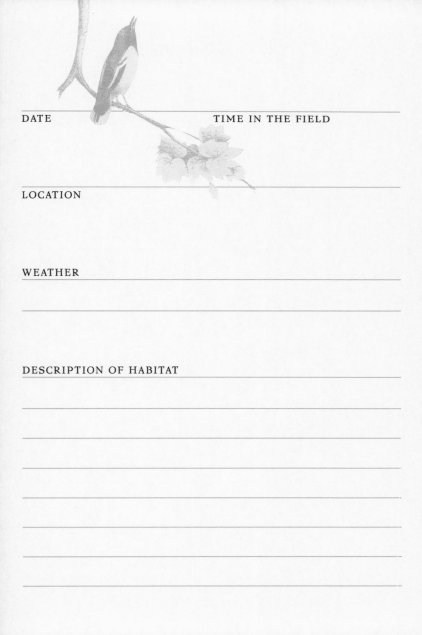

DATE   TIME IN THE FIELD

LOCATION

WEATHER

DESCRIPTION OF HABITAT

Species Observed

_____   _____
_____   _____
_____   _____
_____   _____
_____   _____
_____   _____
_____   _____
_____   _____
_____   _____
_____   _____
_____   _____
_____   _____
_____   _____
_____   _____
_____   _____
_____   _____
_____   _____
_____   _____

BIRDSONG DESCRIPTIONS

_____

_____

_____

_____

FIELD NOTES

_____

_____

_____

_____

_____

_____

_____

_____

_____

_____

_____

_____

_____

_____

DATE   TIME IN THE FIELD

LOCATION

WEATHER

DESCRIPTION OF HABITAT

Species Observed

BIRDSONG DESCRIPTIONS

_____

_____

_____

_____

FIELD NOTES

_____

_____

_____

_____

_____

_____

_____

_____

_____

_____

_____

_____

_____

O birds, your perfect virtues bring,

Your song, your forms, your rhythmic flight,

Your manners for the heart's delight,

Nestle in hedge, or barn, or roof,

Here weave your chamber weather-proof,

Forgive our harms, and condescend

To man, as to a lubber friend,

And, generous, teach his awkward race

Courage, and probity, and grace!

—RALPH WALDO EMERSON

DATE   TIME IN THE FIELD

LOCATION

WEATHER

DESCRIPTION OF HABITAT

Species Observed

BIRDSONG DESCRIPTIONS

_____
_____
_____
_____

FIELD NOTES

_____
_____
_____
_____
_____
_____
_____
_____
_____
_____
_____
_____
_____
_____

DATE   TIME IN THE FIELD

_____

LOCATION

_____

WEATHER

_____

_____

DESCRIPTION OF HABITAT

_____

_____

_____

_____

_____

_____

_____

_____

Species Observed

BIRDSONG DESCRIPTIONS

_____

_____

_____

_____

FIELD NOTES

_____

_____

_____

_____

_____

_____

_____

_____

_____

_____

_____

_____

_____

DATE   TIME IN THE FIELD

LOCATION

WEATHER

DESCRIPTION OF HABITAT

Species Observed

BIRDSONG DESCRIPTIONS

_____

_____

_____

_____

FIELD NOTES

_____

_____

_____

_____

_____

_____

_____

_____

_____

_____

_____

_____

_____

_____

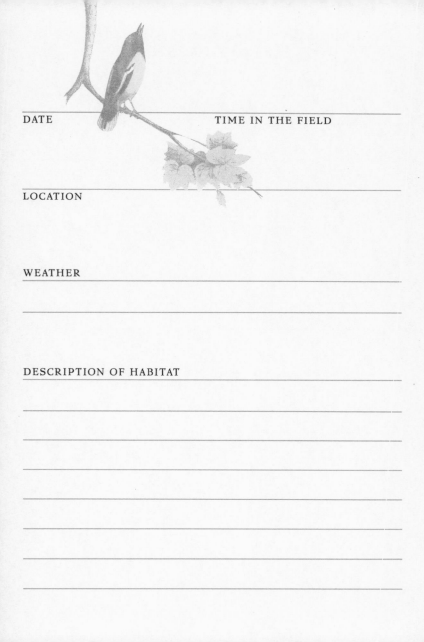

DATE   TIME IN THE FIELD

LOCATION

WEATHER

DESCRIPTION OF HABITAT

Species Observed

_____   _____
_____   _____
_____   _____
_____   _____
_____   _____
_____   _____
_____   _____
_____   _____
_____   _____
_____   _____
_____   _____
_____   _____
_____   _____
_____   _____
_____   _____
_____   _____
_____   _____
_____   _____

BIRDSONG DESCRIPTIONS

_____

_____

_____

_____

FIELD NOTES

_____

_____

_____

_____

_____

_____

_____

_____

_____

_____

_____

_____

_____

_____

DATE _____ TIME IN THE FIELD _____

LOCATION _____

WEATHER _____

_____

DESCRIPTION OF HABITAT _____

_____

_____

_____

_____

_____

_____

_____

Species Observed

_____   _____
_____   _____
_____   _____
_____   _____
_____   _____
_____   _____
_____   _____
_____   _____
_____   _____
_____   _____
_____   _____
_____   _____
_____   _____
_____   _____
_____   _____
_____   _____
_____   _____
_____   _____

BIRDSONG DESCRIPTIONS

_____

_____

_____

_____

FIELD NOTES

_____

_____

_____

_____

_____

_____

_____

_____

_____

_____

_____

_____

_____

FEATHER WEIGHT

- Weighing less than a nickel and measuring three inches long, the calliope humming-bird is the lightest and smallest bird in North America.

- The ostrich is the world's heaviest and tallest bird, weighing in at around three hundred pounds and standing about nine feet high. The weight of an ostrich egg is equivalent to the weight of twenty-four chicken eggs.

- The trumpeter swan is North America's heaviest bird at over forty pounds.

- The whistling swan possesses the greatest number of feathers, featuring 25,216, while the ruby-throated hummingbird has the least amount with around 940 feathers.

- The American white pelican has the longest wingspan, at nine feet, of any bird regularly seen in North American. The wandering albatross seen once in California, however, has a wingspan of eleven feet.

DATE _____ TIME IN THE FIELD _____

LOCATION _____

WEATHER _____
_____

DESCRIPTION OF HABITAT _____
_____
_____
_____
_____
_____
_____
_____

Species Observed

BIRDSONG DESCRIPTIONS

_____

_____

_____

_____

FIELD NOTES

_____

_____

_____

_____

_____

_____

_____

_____

_____

_____

_____

_____

_____

DATE   TIME IN THE FIELD

LOCATION

WEATHER

DESCRIPTION OF HABITAT

Species Observed

BIRDSONG DESCRIPTIONS

_____

_____

_____

_____

FIELD NOTES

_____

_____

_____

_____

_____

_____

_____

_____

_____

_____

_____

_____

_____

DATE _____ TIME IN THE FIELD _____

LOCATION _____

WEATHER _____

_____

DESCRIPTION OF HABITAT _____

_____

_____

_____

_____

_____

_____

_____

Species Observed

BIRDSONG DESCRIPTIONS

_____

_____

_____

_____

FIELD NOTES

_____

_____

_____

_____

_____

_____

_____

_____

_____

_____

_____

_____

_____

_____

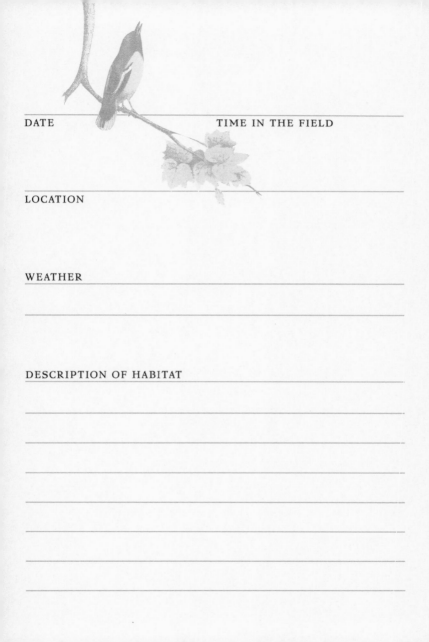

DATE   TIME IN THE FIELD

LOCATION

WEATHER

DESCRIPTION OF HABITAT

Species Observed

_____   _____

_____   _____

_____   _____

_____   _____

_____   _____

_____   _____

_____   _____

_____   _____

_____   _____

_____   _____

_____   _____

_____   _____

_____   _____

_____   _____

_____   _____

_____   _____

_____   _____

_____   _____

_____   _____

BIRDSONG DESCRIPTIONS

_____

_____

_____

_____

FIELD NOTES

_____

_____

_____

_____

_____

_____

_____

_____

_____

_____

_____

_____

_____

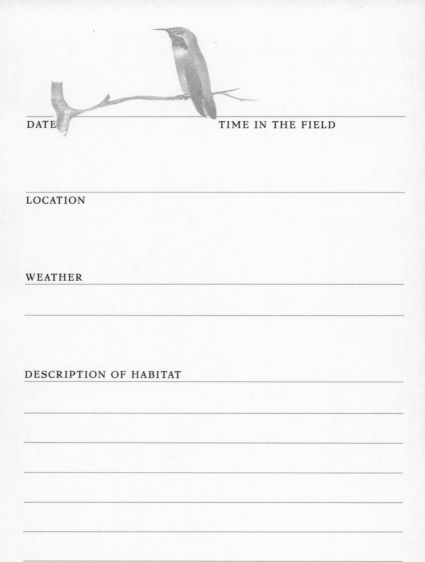

DATE   TIME IN THE FIELD

LOCATION

WEATHER

DESCRIPTION OF HABITAT

Species Observed

_____   _____
_____   _____
_____   _____
_____   _____
_____   _____
_____   _____
_____   _____
_____   _____
_____   _____
_____   _____
_____   _____
_____   _____
_____   _____
_____   _____
_____   _____
_____   _____
_____   _____
_____   _____

BIRDSONG DESCRIPTIONS

_____

_____

_____

_____

FIELD NOTES

_____

_____

_____

_____

_____

_____

_____

_____

_____

_____

_____

_____

_____

A Bird came down the Walk —

He did not know I saw —

He bit an Angleworm in halves

And ate the fellow, raw,

And then he drank a Dew

From a convenient Grass —

And then hopped sidewise to the Wall

To let a Beetle pass

—EMILY DICKINSON

DATE _____ TIME IN THE FIELD _____

LOCATION _____

_____

WEATHER _____

_____

DESCRIPTION OF HABITAT _____

_____

_____

_____

_____

_____

_____

_____

Species Observed

BIRDSONG DESCRIPTIONS

_____

_____

_____

_____

FIELD NOTES

_____

_____

_____

_____

_____

_____

_____

_____

_____

_____

_____

_____

_____

_____

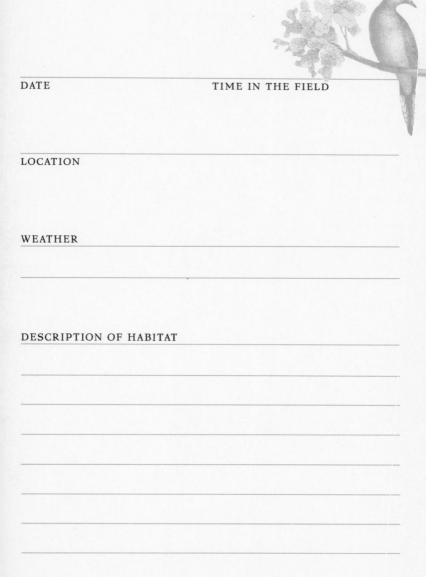

DATE   TIME IN THE FIELD

LOCATION

WEATHER

DESCRIPTION OF HABITAT

Species Observed

BIRDSONG DESCRIPTIONS

_____

_____

_____

_____

FIELD NOTES

_____

_____

_____

_____

_____

_____

_____

_____

_____

_____

_____

_____

_____

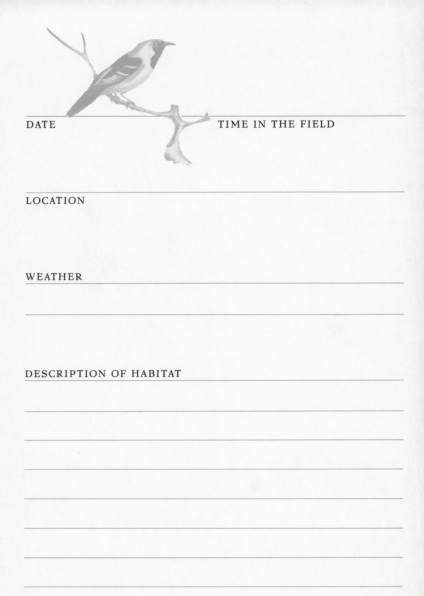

DATE _____ TIME IN THE FIELD _____

LOCATION _____

WEATHER _____

_____

DESCRIPTION OF HABITAT _____

_____

_____

_____

_____

_____

_____

_____

Species Observed

BIRDSONG DESCRIPTIONS

_____

_____

_____

_____

FIELD NOTES

_____

_____

_____

_____

_____

_____

_____

_____

_____

_____

_____

_____

_____

_____

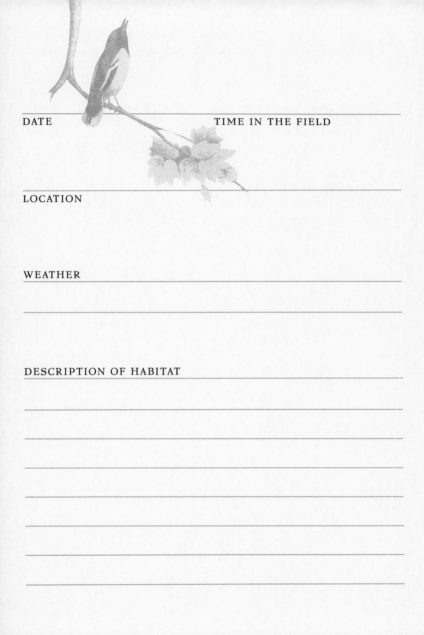

DATE   TIME IN THE FIELD

LOCATION

WEATHER

DESCRIPTION OF HABITAT

Species Observed

_____   _____
_____   _____
_____   _____
_____   _____
_____   _____
_____   _____
_____   _____
_____   _____
_____   _____
_____   _____
_____   _____
_____   _____
_____   _____
_____   _____
_____   _____
_____   _____
_____   _____
_____   _____

BIRDSONG DESCRIPTIONS

_____

_____

_____

_____

FIELD NOTES

_____

_____

_____

_____

_____

_____

_____

_____

_____

_____

_____

_____

_____

_____

DATE _____ TIME IN THE FIELD _____

LOCATION _____

WEATHER _____

_____

DESCRIPTION OF HABITAT _____

_____

_____

_____

_____

_____

_____

Species Observed

BIRDSONG DESCRIPTIONS

_____

_____

_____

_____

FIELD NOTES

_____

_____

_____

_____

_____

_____

_____

_____

_____

_____

_____

_____

_____

_____

BIRDS OF PASSAGE Species Observed

- The roadrunner is the world's fastest running flying bird, reaching foot speeds of up to 26 mph.

- The ostrich is the fastest running non-flying bird in the world. It can sprint in short bursts of up to 43 mph and can maintain a steady speed of 31 mph.

- The peregrine falcon is the fastest bird in the world. It regularly attains speeds of 40–60 mph and has been clocked in at 175 mph when diving from great heights.

- The American woodcock is the slowest-flying North American bird, averaging 5 mph during flight.

- Hummingbirds (namely the amethyst woodstar and horned sungem) beat their wings the fastest at 90 beats per second. Vultures beat their wings the slowest at 1 beat per second.

- The gentoo penguin is the world's fastest underwater swimming bird, attaining speeds of 22.3 mph.

- The sooty tern can fly for 3 to 10 years without landing, but the longest round trip migration belongs to the Arctic tern at 25,000 miles.

ORNITHOLOGICAL MISCELLANY

- The record for the greatest weight-carrying capacity belongs to the bald eagle, with its ability to carry a fifteen-pound mule deer.

- The marsh warbler can sing up to eighty-four songs, making it the greatest bird mimic in the world.

- The eagle was the first bird to be featured on the U.S. postage stamp.

- Benjamin Franklin thought the wild turkey was the best choice for America's national bird.

- Flamingos and swans were once considered delicacies by the wealthy but have since been protected.

- Blue jays are actually gray. A light refraction causes an optical illusion, making the gray feathers seem blue.

- Sparrows came to the United States from Europe in the 1800s and spread rapidly, becoming one of the most populous birds in North America.

Cuckoo.

Cuckoo.

Cuckoo.

SKETCHES AND PHOTOGRAPHS

Black-billed Cuckoo.

Great Spotted Cuckoo.

Yellow-billed Cuckoo.

Cuckoo.

Cuckoo.

Cuckoo.

Cuckoo.

Cuckoo.

FAMILY.	GENUS.	SPECIES.	SUBSPECIES.	ENGLISH NAMES.	A. O. U. No.	PAGE.
dæ. Crows, Jays, Magpies, etc.	Perisoreus	canadensis		Canada Jay	484	9
			capitalis	Rocky Mountain Jay	484a	17
			fumifrons	Alaskan Jay	484b	
			nigricapillus	Labrador Jay	484c	
		obscurus		Oregon Jay	485	17
	Corvus	corax	sinuatus	Mexican Raven	486	9
			principalis	Northern Raven	486a	
		cryptoleucus		White-necked Raven	487	17
		americanus		American Crow	488	9
			floridanus	Florida Crow	488a	16
			hesperis	California Crow	488b	
		caurinus		Northwest Crow	489	16
		ossifragus		Fish Crow	490	16
	Picicorvus	columbianus		Clarke's Nutcracker	491	16
	Cyanocephalus	cyanocephalus		Piñon Jay	492	13
dæ. Starlings	Sturnus	vulgaris		Starling	493	
dæ. Blackbirds, Orioles, etc.	Dolichonyx	oryzivorus		Bobolink	494	47
			albinucha	Western Bobolink	494a	
	Molothrus	ater		Cowbird	495	78
			obscurus	Dwarf Cowbird	495a	172
	Callothrus	robustus		Bronzed Cowbird	496	
	Xanthocephalus	xanthocephalus		Yellow-headed Blackbird	497	101
	Agelaius	phœniceus		Red-winged Blackbird	498	44
			briyanti	Bahaman Red-wing	498a	
			sonoriensis	Sonoran Red-wing	498b	
		gubernator		Bicolored Blackbird	499	155
		tricolor		Tricolored Blackbird	500	110
				...lark	501	23
				...adowlark	501a	
				...dowlark	501b	155
					502	
				...iole	503	164
					504	172
				...ble	505	148
				...ooded Oriole	505a	
		spurius		Orchard Oriole	506	13
		galbula		Baltimore Oriole	507	12
		bullocki		Bullock's Oriole	508	136
	Scolecophagus	carolinus		Rusty Blackbird	509	78
		cyanocephalus		Brewer's Blackbird	510	92
	Quiscalus	quiscula		Purple Grackle	511	77
			aglæus	Florida Grackle	511a	77
			æneus	Bronzed Grackle	511b	172
		macrourus		Great-tailed Grackle	512	165
		major		Boat-tailed Grackle	513	77
lidæ. Finches, Sparrows, etc.	Coccothraustes	vespertina		Evening Grosbeak	514	133
	Pinicola	enucleator		Pine Grosbeak	515	54
			kadiaka	Kadiak Pine Grosbeak	515a	
	Pyrrhula	cassini		Cassin's Bullfinch	516	172
	Carpodacus	purpureus		Purple Finch	517	69
			californicus	California Purple Finch	517a	
		cassini		Cassin's Purple Finch	518	144
		mexicanus	frontalis	House Finch	519	108
		amplus		Guadalupe House Finch	520	
	Loxia	curvirostra	minor	American Crossbill	521	53
			stricklandi	Mexican Crossbill	521a	138
		leucoptera		White-winged Crossbill	522	79
	Leucosticte	griseonucha		Aleutian Leucosticte	523	135
		tephrocotis		Gray-crowned Leucosticte	524	
			littoralis	Hepburn's Leucosticte	524a	
		atrata		Black Leucosticte	525	
		australis		Brown-capped Leucosticte	526	135
	Acanthis	hornemannii		Greenland Redpoll	527	
			exilipes	Hoary Redpoll	527a	104
		linaria		Redpoll	528	69
			holbœllii	Holbœll's Redpoll	528a	
			rostrata	Greater Redpoll	528b	
	Spinus	tristis		American Goldfinch	529	68
		psaltria		Arkansas Goldfinch	530	130
			arizonæ	Arizona Goldfinch	530a	172
			mexicanus	Mexican Goldfinch	530b	172
		lawrencei		Lawrence's Goldfinch	531	131
		notatus		Black-headed Goldfinch	532	132
		pinus		Pine Siskin	533	157
	Plectrophenax	nivalis		Snowflake	534	11
			townsendi	Prybilof Snowflake	534a	
		hyperboreus		McKay's Snowflake	535	
	Calcarius	lapponicus		Lapland Longspur	536	

Species Checklist

This checklist is taken from *The Sibley Guide to Bird Life and Behavior* by The National Audubon Society and David Allen Sibley and includes species that have been reported in the United States (excluding Hawaii) and Canada. This is not an official checklist for the region, as the list includes many introduced species that are not considered established, as well as several species that have been recently reported in North America but are not yet accepted by the appropriate checklist committees. Check boxes appear next to the species that are included in the main American Ornithologists' Union (AOU) Check-list for the region, as well as next to introduced species if they are considered established by the AOU; species that have not been officially accepted are denoted by italic type.

The scientific and common names of each order and family appear in the list below, followed by the common name of each species in the family. Accidental species (birds that very rarely occur in the United States or Canada and are only present due to unnatural or fortuitous circumstances) are identified by an (A) after the species name, introduced or escaped species by an (I), and extinct species by an (E). The AOU checklist is continually being revised as new species are reported and reviewed, as the status of introduced species changes, and as taxonomic changes are evaluated. For the most up-to-date AOU Check-list, please visit the website www.aou.org.

Family / Species   Date / Location Seen

GAVIIFORMES
Loons
LOONS (*GAVIIDAE*)

- ❏ Red-throated Loon _____
- ❏ Arctic Loon _____
- ❏ Pacific Loon _____
- ❏ Common Loon _____
- ❏ Yellow-billed Loon _____

PODICIPEDIFORMES
Grebes
GREBES (*PODICIPEDIDAE*)

- ❏ Least Grebe _____
- ❏ Pied-billed Grebe _____
- ❏ Horned Grebe _____
- ❏ Red-necked Grebe _____
- ❏ Eared Grebe _____
- ❏ Western Grebe _____
- ❏ Clark's Grebe _____

PROCELLARIIFORMES
Tubenoses
ALBATROSSES (*DIOMEDEIDAE*)

- ❏ Yellow-nosed Albatross (A) _____
- ❏ Shy Albatross (A) _____
- ❏ Black-browed Albatross (A) _____
- ❏ Light-mantled Albatross (A) _____

Family / Species	Date / Location Seen

❑ Wandering Albatross (A) _____
❑ Laysan Albatross _____
❑ Black-footed Albatross _____
❑ Short-tailed Albatross _____

SHEARWATERS AND PETRELS (*PROCELLARIIDAE*)

❑ Northern Fulmar _____
❑ Herald Petrel _____
❑ Murphy's Petrel _____
   Great-winged Petrel (A) _____
❑ Mottled Petrel _____
❑ Bermuda Petrel (A) _____
   Fea's Petrel _____
❑ Black-capped Petrel _____
❑ Dark-rumped Petrel (A) _____
❑ Cook's Petrel _____
❑ Stejneger's Petrel (A) _____
   Bulwer's Petrel (A) _____
   White-chinned Petrel (A) _____
   Parkinson's Petrel (A) _____
❑ Streaked Shearwater (A) _____
❑ Cory's Shearwater _____
❑ Pink-footed Shearwater _____
❑ Flesh-footed Shearwater _____
❑ Greater Shearwater _____
❑ Wedge-tailed Shearwater (A) _____
❑ Buller's Shearwater _____

Family / Species	Date / Location Seen

❏ Sooty Shearwater _____

❏ Short-tailed Shearwater _____

❏ Manx Shearwater _____

❏ Black-vented Shearwater _____

❏ Audubon's Shearwater _____

❏ Little Shearwater (A) _____

STORM-PETRELS (*HYDROBATIDAE*)

❏ Wilson's Storm-Petrel _____

❏ White-faced Storm-Petrel _____

❏ European Storm-Petrel (A) _____

❏ Fork-tailed Storm-Petrel _____

❏ Leach's Storm-Petrel _____

  Swinhoe's Storm-Petrel (A) _____

❏ Ashy Storm-Petrel _____

❏ Band-rumped Storm-Petrel _____

❏ Wedge-rumped Storm-Petrel (A) _____

❏ Black Storm-Petrel _____

  Markham's Storm-Petrel (A) _____

❏ Least Storm-Petrel _____

PELECANIFORMES

Totipalmate Birds

TROPICBIRDS (*PHAETHONTIDAE*)

❏ White-tailed Tropicbird _____

❏ Red-billed Tropicbird _____

❏ Red-tailed Tropicbird (A) _____

Family / Species	Date / Location Seen

BOOBIES AND GANNETS (*SULIDAE*)

❏ Masked Booby _____

❏ Blue-footed Booby _____

❏ Brown Booby _____

❏ Red-footed Booby _____

❏ Northern Gannet _____

PELICANS (*PELECANIDAE*)

❏ American White Pelican _____

❏ Brown Pelican _____

CORMORANTS (*PHALACROCORACIDAE*)

❏ Brandt's Cormorant _____

❏ Neotropic Cormorant _____

❏ Double-crested Cormorant _____

❏ Great Cormorant _____

❏ Red-faced Cormorant _____

❏ Pelagic Cormorant _____

DARTERS (ANHINGA) (*ANHINGIDAE*)

❏ Anhinga _____

FRIGATEBIRDS (*FREGATIDAE*)

❏ Magnificent Frigatebird _____

❏ Great Frigatebird (A) _____

❏ Lesser Frigatebird (A) _____

Family / Species   Date / Location Seen

CICONIIFORMES

Heron, Ibises, Storks, New World Vultures, and Allies

HERONS, EGRETS, AND BITTERNS (*ARDEIDAE*)

❏ American Bittern _____

❏ Yellow Bittern (A) _____

❏ Least Bittern _____

❏ Great Blue Heron _____

❏ Great Egret _____

❏ Chinese Egret (A) _____

❏ Little Egret _____

❏ Western Reef-Heron (A) _____

❏ Snowy Egret _____

❏ Little Blue Heron _____

❏ Tricolored Heron _____

❏ Reddish Egret _____

❏ Cattle Egret _____

❏ Chinese Pond-Heron (A) _____

❏ Green Heron _____

❏ Black-crowned Night-Heron _____

❏ Yellow-crowned Night-Heron _____

IBISES AND SPOONBILLS (*THRESKIORNITHIDAE*)

❏ White Ibis _____

❏ Scarlet Ibis _____

❏ Glossy Ibis _____

❏ White-faced Ibis _____

❏ Roseate Spoonbill _____

Family / Species	Date / Location Seen

STORKS (*CICONIIDAE*)
- ☐ Jabiru (A) _____
- ☐ Wood Stork _____

NEW WORLD VULTURES (*CATHARTIDAE*)
- ☐ Black Vulture _____
- ☐ Turkey Vulture _____
- ☐ California Condor _____

PHOENICOPTERIFORMES
Flamingos
FLAMINGOS (*PHOENICOPTERIDAE*)
- ☐ Greater Flamingo _____

ANSERIFORMES
Ducks, Geese, and Swans
DUCKS, GEESE, AND SWANS (*ANATIDAE*)
- ☐ Black-bellied Whistling-Duck _____
- *West Indian Whistling-Duck (I)* _____
- ☐ Fulvous Whistling-Duck _____
- ☐ Bean Goose (A) _____
- ☐ Pink-footed Goose (A) _____
- ☐ Greater White-fronted Goose _____
- ☐ Lesser White-fronted Goose (A) _____
- ☐ Emperor Goose _____
- ☐ Snow Goose _____
- ☐ Ross's Goose _____

Family / Species	Date / Location Seen

❑ Canada Goose _____

 Red-breasted Goose (I) _____

❑ Brant _____

❑ Barnacle Goose _____

 Ruddy Shelduck (I) _____

 Common Shelduck (I) _____

❑ Mute Swan (I) _____

❑ Trumpeter Swan _____

❑ Tundra Swan _____

❑ Whooper Swan _____

❑ Muscovy Duck _____

❑ Wood Duck _____

 Mandarin Duck (I) _____

❑ Gadwall _____

❑ Falcated Duck (A) _____

❑ Eurasian Wigeon _____

❑ American Wigeon _____

❑ American Black Duck _____

❑ Mallard _____

❑ Mottled Duck _____

❑ Spot-billed Duck (A) _____

❑ Blue-winged Teal _____

❑ Cinnamon Teal _____

❑ Northern Shoveler _____

❑ White-cheeked Pintail (A) _____

❑ Northern Pintail _____

❑ Garganey _____

Family / Species	Date / Location Seen
❏ Baikal Teal (A)	_____
❏ Green-winged Teal	_____
❏ Canvasback	_____
❏ Redhead	_____
❏ Common Pochard (A)	_____
❏ Ring-necked Duck	_____
❏ Tufted Duck	_____
❏ Greater Scaup	_____
❏ Lesser Scaup	_____
❏ Steller's Eider	_____
❏ Spectacled Eider	_____
❏ King Eider	_____
❏ Common Eider	_____
❏ Harlequin Duck	_____
Labrador Duck (E)	_____
❏ Surf Scoter	_____
❏ White-winged Scoter	_____
❏ Black Scoter	_____
❏ Long-tailed Duck	_____
❏ Bufflehead	_____
❏ Common Goldeneye	_____
❏ Barrow's Goldeneye	_____
❏ Smew (A)	_____
❏ Hooded Merganser	_____
❏ Common Merganser	_____
❏ Red-breasted Merganser	_____
❏ Masked Duck	_____
❏ Ruddy Duck	_____

Family / Species   Date / Location Seen

FALCONIFORMES
Diurnal Birds of Prey
HAWKS AND ALLIES (*ACCIPITRIDAE*)

❑ Osprey _____

❑ Hook-billed Kite _____

❑ Swallow-tailed Kite _____

❑ White-tailed Kite _____

❑ Snail Kite _____

❑ Mississippi Kite _____

❑ Bald Eagle _____

❑ White-tailed Eagle (A)_____

❑ Steller's Sea-Eagle (A) _____

❑ Northern Harrier _____

❑ Sharp-shinned Hawk _____

❑ Cooper's Hawk _____

❑ Northern Goshawk _____

❑ Crane Hawk (A) _____

❑ Gray Hawk _____

❑ Common Black-Hawk _____

❑ Harris's Hawk _____

❑ Roadside Hawk (A) _____

❑ Red-shouldered Hawk _____

❑ Broad-winged Hawk _____

❑ Short-tailed Hawk _____

❑ Swainson's Hawk _____

❑ White-tailed Hawk _____

❑ Zone-tailed Hawk _____

❑ Red-tailed Hawk _____

Family / Species	Date / Location Seen

- ❏ Ferruginous Hawk _____
- ❏ Rough-legged Hawk _____
- ❏ Golden Eagle _____

FALCONS AND CARACARAS (*FALCONIDAE*)
- ❏ Collared Forest-Falcon (A) _____
- ❏ Crested Caracara _____
- ❏ Eurasian Kestrel (A) _____
- ❏ American Kestrel _____
- ❏ Merlin _____
- ❏ Eurasian Hobby (A) _____
- ❏ Aplomado Falcon _____
- ❏ Gyrfalcon _____
- ❏ Peregrine Falcon _____
- ❏ Prairie Falcon _____

GALLIFORMES

Gallinaceous Birds

CHACHALACAS AND ALLIES (*CRACIDAE*)
- ❏ Plain Chachalaca _____

GROUSE, TURKEYS, AND ALLIES (*PHASIANIDAE*)
- ❏ Chukar (I) _____
- *Red-legged Partridge (I)* _____
- *Black Francolin (I)* _____
- ❏ Himalayan Snowcock (I) _____
- ❏ Gray Partridge (I) _____
- ❏ Ring-necked Pheasant (I) _____

Family / Species	Date / Location Seen

Common Peafowl (I) _____

❏ Ruffed Grouse _____
❏ Greater Sage-Grouse _____
❏ Gunnison Sage-Grouse _____
❏ Spruce Grouse _____
❏ Willow Ptarmigan _____
❏ Rock Ptarmigan _____
❏ White-tailed Ptarmigan _____
❏ Blue Grouse _____
❏ Sharp-tailed Grouse _____
❏ Greater Prairie-Chicken _____
❏ Lesser Prairie-Chicken _____
❏ Wild Turkey _____
Helmeted Guineafowl (I) _____

NEW WORLD QUAIL (*ODONTOPHORIDAE*)

❏ Mountain Quail _____
❏ Scaled Quail _____
❏ California Quail _____
❏ Gambel's Quail _____
❏ Northern Bobwhite _____
❏ Montezuma Quail _____

GRUIFORMES
Rails, Cranes, and Allies
RAILS, GALLINULES, AND COOTS (*RALLIDAE*)

❏ Yellow Rail _____
❏ Black Rail _____

Family / Species	Date / Location Seen

❏   Corn Crake (A) _____

❏   Clapper Rail _____

❏   King Rail _____

❏   Virginia Rail _____

       Baillon's Crake (A) _____

❏   Sora _____

❏   Paint-billed Crake (A) _____

❏   Spotted Rail (A) _____

       Purple Swamphen (I) _____

❏   Purple Gallinule _____

❏   Azure Gallinule (A) _____

❏   Common Moorhen _____

❏   Eurasian Coot (A)_____

❏   American Coot _____

LIMPKIN (*ARAMIDAE*)

❏   Limpkin _____

CRANES (*GRUIDAE*)

❏   Sandhill Crane _____

❏   Common Crane (A) _____

❏   Whooping Crane _____

CHARADRIIFORMES

Shorebirds, Gulls, Auks, and Allies

THICK-KNEES (*BURHINIDAE*)

❏   Double-striped Thick-knee (A) _____

Family / Species	Date / Location Seen

PLOVERS AND LAPWINGS (*CHARADRIIDAE*)

- ❏ Northern Lapwing _____
- ❏ Black-bellied Plover _____
- ❏ European Golden-Plover _____
- ❏ American Golden-Plover _____
- ❏ Pacific Golden-Plover _____
- ❏ Mongolian Plover _____
- ❏ Collared Plover (A) _____
- ❏ Snowy Plover _____
- ❏ Wilson's Plover _____
- ❏ Common Ringed Plover _____
- ❏ Semipalmated Plover _____
- ❏ Piping Plover _____
- ❏ Little Ringed Plover (A) _____
- ❏ Killdeer _____
- ❏ Mountain Plover _____
- ❏ Eurasian Dotterel _____

OYSTERCATCHERS (*HAEMATOPODIDAE*)

- ❏ Eurasian Oystercatcher (A) _____
- ❏ American Oystercatcher _____
- ❏ Black Oystercatcher _____

STILTS AND AVOCETS (*RECURVIROSTRIDAE*)

- ❏ Black-winged Stilt (A) _____
- ❏ Black-necked Stilt _____
- ❏ American Avocet _____

Family / Species	Date / Location Seen

JACANAS (*JACANIDAE*)

❏ Northern Jacana _____

SANDPIPERS, PHALAROPES, AND ALLIES (*SCOLOPACIDAE*)

❏ Common Greenshank (A) _____
❏ Greater Yellowlegs _____
❏ Lesser Yellowlegs _____
❏ Marsh Sandpiper (A) _____
❏ Common Redshank (A) _____
❏ Spotted Redshank _____
❏ Wood Sandpiper (A)_____
❏ Green Sandpiper (A) _____
❏ Solitary Sandpiper _____
❏ Willet _____
❏ Wandering Tattler _____
❏ Gray-tailed Tattler (A) _____
❏ Common Sandpiper (A)_____
❏ Spotted Sandpiper _____
❏ Terek Sandpiper (A)_____
❏ Upland Sandpiper _____
❏ Little Curlew (A) _____
❏ Eskimo Curlew (E?)_____
❏ Whimbrel _____
❏ Bristle-thighed Curlew _____
❏ Far Eastern Curlew (A) _____
❏ Slender-billed Curlew (A) _____
❏ Eurasian Curlew (A) _____

Family / Species   Date / Location Seen

- ❏ Long-billed Curlew _____
- ❏ Black-tailed Godwit _____
- ❏ Hudsonian Godwit _____
- ❏ Bar-tailed Godwit _____
- ❏ Marbled Godwit _____
- ❏ Ruddy Turnstone _____
- ❏ Black Turnstone _____
- ❏ Surfbird _____
- ❏ Great Knot (A) _____
- ❏ Red Knot _____
- ❏ Sanderling _____
- ❏ Semipalmated Sandpiper _____
- ❏ Western Sandpiper _____
- ❏ Red-necked Stint _____
- ❏ Little Stint _____
- ❏ Temminck's Stint (A) _____
- ❏ Long-toed Stint (A) _____
- ❏ Least Sandpiper _____
- ❏ White-rumped Sandpiper _____
- ❏ Baird's Sandpiper _____
- ❏ Pectoral Sandpiper _____
- ❏ Sharp-tailed Sandpiper _____
- ❏ Purple Sandpiper _____
- ❏ Rock Sandpiper _____
- ❏ Dunlin _____
- ❏ Curlew Sandpiper _____
- ❏ Stilt Sandpiper _____

Family / Species   Date / Location Seen

- ❏ Spoon-billed Sandpiper (A) _____
- ❏ Broad-billed Sandpiper (A) _____
- ❏ Buff-breasted Sandpiper _____
- ❏ Ruff _____
- ❏ Short-billed Dowitcher _____
- ❏ Long-billed Dowitcher _____
- ❏ Jack Snipe (A) _____
- ❏ Common Snipe _____
- ❏ Pin-tailed Snipe (A) _____
- ❏ Eurasian Woodcock (A) _____
- ❏ American Woodcock _____
- ❏ Wilson's Phalarope _____
- ❏ Red-necked Phalarope _____
- ❏ Red Phalarope _____

COURSERS AND PRATINCOLES (*GLAREOLIDAE*)

- ❏ Oriental Pratincole (A) _____

GULLS, TERNS, AND ALLIES (*LARIDAE*)

- ❏ Great Skua _____
- ❏ South Polar Skua _____
- ❏ Pomarine Jaeger _____
- ❏ Parasitic Jaeger _____
- ❏ Long-tailed Jaeger _____
- ❏ Laughing Gull _____
- ❏ Franklin's Gull _____
- ❏ Little Gull _____

Family / Species   Date / Location Seen

- ❏ Black-headed Gull _____
- ❏ Bonaparte's Gull _____
- _Gray-hooded Gull (A)_ _____
- ❏ Heermann's Gull _____
- ❏ Gray Gull (A) _____
- ❏ Band-tailed Gull (A) _____
- ❏ Black-tailed Gull _____
- ❏ Mew Gull _____
- ❏ Ring-billed Gull _____
- _Kelp Gull_ _____
- ❏ California Gull _____
- ❏ Herring Gull _____
- ❏ Yellow-legged Gull _____
- ❏ Thayer's Gull _____
- ❏ Iceland Gull _____
- ❏ Lesser Black-backed Gull _____
- ❏ Slaty-backed Gull _____
- ❏ Yellow-footed Gull _____
- ❏ Western Gull _____
- ❏ Glaucous-winged Gull _____
- ❏ Glaucous Gull _____
- ❏ Great Black-backed Gull _____
- ❏ Sabine's Gull _____
- _Swallow-tailed Gull (A)_ _____
- ❏ Black-legged Kittiwake _____
- ❏ Red-legged Kittiwake _____
- ❏ Ross's Gull _____

Family / Species	Date / Location Seen

❏ Ivory Gull _____

❏ Gull-billed Tern _____

❏ Caspian Tern _____

❏ Royal Tern _____

❏ Elegant Tern _____

❏ Sandwich Tern _____

❏ Roseate Tern _____

❏ Common Tern _____

❏ Arctic Tern _____

❏ Forster's Tern _____

❏ Least Tern _____

❏ Aleutian Tern _____

❏ Bridled Tern _____

❏ Sooty Tern _____

❏ Large-billed Tern (A) _____

❏ White-winged Tern _____

❏ Whiskered Tern (A) _____

❏ Black Tern _____

❏ Brown Noddy _____

❏ Black Noddy _____

❏ Black Skimmer _____

AUKS (*ALCIDAE*)

❏ Dovekie _____

❏ Common Murre _____

❏ Thick-billed Murre _____

❏ Razorbill _____

Family / Species	Date / Location Seen

Great Auk (E) _____

❏ Black Guillemot _____

❏ Pigeon Guillemot _____

❏ Long-billed Murrelet _____

❏ Marbled Murrelet _____

❏ Kittlitz's Murrelet _____

❏ Xantus's Murrelet _____

❏ Craveri's Murrelet _____

❏ Ancient Murrelet _____

❏ Cassin's Auklet _____

❏ Parakeet Auklet _____

❏ Least Auklet _____

❏ Whiskered Auklet _____

❏ Crested Auklet _____

❏ Rhinoceros Auklet _____

❏ Atlantic Puffin _____

❏ Horned Puffin _____

❏ Tufted Puffin _____

COLUMBIFORMES

Pigeons and Doves

PIGEONS AND DOVES (*COLUMBIDAE*)

❏ Rock Dove (I) _____

❏ Scaly-naped Pigeon (A) _____

❏ White-crowned Pigeon _____

❏ Red-billed Pigeon _____

❏ Band-tailed Pigeon _____

Family / Species	Date / Location Seen

- ❏ Oriental Turtle-Dove (A) _____
- ❏ Ringed Turtle-Dove (I) _____
- ❏ European Turtle-Dove (A) _____
- ❏ Eurasian Collared-Dove (I) _____
- ❏ Spotted Dove (I) _____
- ❏ White-winged Dove _____
- ❏ Zenaida Dove (A) _____
- ❏ Mourning Dove _____
-    Passenger Pigeon (E) _____
- ❏ Inca Dove _____
- ❏ Common Ground-Dove _____
- ❏ Ruddy Ground-Dove _____
- ❏ White-tipped Dove _____
- ❏ Key West Quail-Dove _____
- ❏ Ruddy Quail-Dove (A) _____

PSITTACIFORMES

Parrots

PARROTS AND ALLIES (*PSITTACIDAE*)

-    *Sulphur-crested Cockatoo (I)* _____
-    *Cockatiel (I)* _____
- ❏ Budgerigar (I) _____
-    *Peach-faced Lovebird (I)* _____
- ❏ Rose-ringed Parakeet (I) _____
- ❏ Monk Parakeet (I) _____
-    Carolina Parakeet (E) _____
-    *Blue-crowned Parakeet (I)* _____

Family / Species	Date / Location Seen

❑ Green Parakeet (I) _____

Mitred Parakeet (I) _____

Red-masked Parakeet (I) _____

Dusky-headed Parakeet (I) _____

Black-hooded Parakeet (I) _____

Chestnut-fronted Macaw (I) _____

❑ Thick-billed Parrot _____

❑ White-winged Parakeet (I) _____

Yellow-chevroned Parakeet (I) _____

White-fronted Parrot (I) _____

Yellow-lored Parrot (I) _____

Hispaniolan Parrot (I) _____

❑ Red-crowned Parrot (I) _____

Lilac-crowned Parrot (I) _____

Red-lored Parrot (I) _____

Blue-fronted Parrot (I) _____

Mealy Parrot (I) _____

Yellow-headed Parrot (I) _____

Yellow-naped Parrot (I) _____

Yellow-crowned Parrot (I) _____

Orange-winged Parrot (I) _____

CUCULIFORMES

Cuckoos and Allies

CUCKOOS, ROADRUNNERS, AND ANIS (*CUCULIDAE*)

❑ Common Cuckoo (A) _____

❑ Oriental Cuckoo (A) _____

Family / Species	Date / Location Seen

❑ Black-billed Cuckoo _____
❑ Yellow-billed Cuckoo _____
❑ Mangrove Cuckoo _____
  Dark-billed Cuckoo (A) _____
❑ Greater Roadrunner _____
❑ Smooth-billed Ani _____
❑ Groove-billed Ani _____

STRIGIFORMES

Owls

BARN OWLS (*TYTONIDAE*)

❑ Barn Owl _____

TYPICAL OWLS (*STRIGIDAE*)

❑ Flammulated Owl _____
❑ Oriental Scops-Owl (A) _____
❑ Western Screech-Owl _____
❑ Eastern Screech-Owl _____
❑ Whiskered Screech-Owl _____
❑ Great Horned Owl _____
❑ Snowy Owl _____
❑ Northern Hawk Owl _____
❑ Northern Pygmy-Owl _____
❑ Ferruginous Pygmy-Owl _____
❑ Elf Owl _____
❑ Burrowing Owl _____
❑ Mottled Owl (A) _____

Family / Species	Date / Location Seen

- ❏ Spotted Owl _____
- ❏ Barred Owl _____
- ❏ Great Gray Owl _____
- ❏ Long-eared Owl _____
- ❏ Stygian Owl (A) _____
- ❏ Short-eared Owl _____
- ❏ Boreal Owl _____
- ❏ Northern Saw-whet Owl _____

CAPRIMULGIFORMES
Goatsuckers and Allies
NIGHTHAWKS AND NIGHTJARS (*CAPRIMULGIDAE*)

- ❏ Lesser Nighthawk _____
- ❏ Common Nighthawk _____
- ❏ Antillean Nighthawk _____
- ❏ Common Pauraque _____
- ❏ Common Poorwill _____
- ❏ Chuck-will's-widow _____
- ❏ Buff-collared Nightjar _____
- ❏ Whip-poor-will _____
- ❏ Jungle Nightjar (A) _____

APODIFORMES
Swifts and Hummingbirds
SWIFTS (*APODIDAE*)

- ❏ Black Swift _____
- ❏ White-collared Swift (A) _____

Family / Species	Date / Location Seen

- ❏ Chimney Swift _____
- ❏ Vaux's Swift _____
- ❏ White-throated Needletail (A) _____
- ❏ Common Swift (A) _____
- ❏ Fork-tailed Swift (A) _____
- ❏ White-throated Swift _____
- ❏ Antillean Palm-Swift (A) _____

HUMMINGBIRDS (*TROCHILIDAE*)

- ❏ Green Violet-ear _____
- ❏ Green-breasted Mango (A) _____
- ❏ Broad-billed Hummingbird _____
- ❏ White-eared Hummingbird _____
- ❏ Xantus's Hummingbird (A) _____
- ❏ Berylline Hummingbird _____
- ❏ Buff-bellied Hummingbird _____
- ❏ Cinnamon Hummingbird (A) _____
- ❏ Violet-crowned Hummingbird _____
- ❏ Blue-throated Hummingbird _____
- ❏ Magnificent Hummingbird _____
- ❏ Plain-capped Starthroat _____
- ❏ Bahama Woodstar (A)_____
- ❏ Lucifer Hummingbird _____
- ❏ Ruby-throated Hummingbird _____
- ❏ Black-chinned Hummingbird _____
- ❏ Anna's Hummingbird _____
- ❏ Costa's Hummingbird _____

Family / Species	Date / Location Seen

- ❏ Calliope Hummingbird _____
- ❏ Bumblebee Hummingbird (A) _____
- ❏ Broad-tailed Hummingbird _____
- ❏ Rufous Hummingbird _____
- ❏ Allen's Hummingbird _____

TROGONIFORMES

Trogons

TROGONS (*TROGONIDAE*)

- ❏ Elegant Trogon _____
- ❏ Eared Trogon _____

UPUPIFORMES

Hoopoes and Allies

HOOPOE (*UPUPIDAE*)

- ❏ Eurasian Hoopoe (A) _____

CORACIIFORMES

Kingfishers and Allies

KINGFISHERS (*ALCEDINIDAE*)

- ❏ Ringed Kingfisher _____
- ❏ Belted Kingfisher _____
- ❏ Green Kingfisher _____

PICIFORMES

Woodpeckers and Allies

WOODPECKERS AND ALLIES (*PICIDAE*)

Family / Species	Date / Location Seen

- ❏ Eurasian Wryneck (A) _____
- ❏ Lewis's Woodpecker _____
- ❏ Red-headed Woodpecker _____
- ❏ Acorn Woodpecker _____
- ❏ Gila Woodpecker _____
- ❏ Golden-fronted Woodpecker _____
- ❏ Red-bellied Woodpecker _____
- ❏ Williamson's Sapsucker _____
- ❏ Yellow-bellied Sapsucker _____
- ❏ Red-naped Sapsucker _____
- ❏ Red-breasted Sapsucker _____
- ❏ Great Spotted Woodpecker (A) _____
- ❏ Ladder-backed Woodpecker _____
- ❏ Nuttall's Woodpecker _____
- ❏ Downy Woodpecker _____
- ❏ Hairy Woodpecker _____
- ❏ Arizona Woodpecker _____
- ❏ Red-cockaded Woodpecker _____
- ❏ White-headed Woodpecker _____
- ❏ Three-toed Woodpecker _____
- ❏ Black-backed Woodpecker _____
- ❏ Northern Flicker _____
- ❏ Gilded Flicker _____
- ❏ Pileated Woodpecker _____
- Ivory-billed Woodpecke (?E) _____

Family / Species	Date / Location Seen

PASSERIFORMES

Passerine Birds

TYRANT FLYCATCHERS (*TYRANNIDAE*)

☐ Northern Beardless-Tyrannulet _____

☐ Greenish Elaenia (A) _____

☐ Caribbean Elaenia (A) _____

☐ Tufted Flycatcher (A) _____

☐ Olive-sided Flycatcher _____

☐ Greater Pewee _____

☐ Western Wood-Pewee _____

☐ Eastern Wood-Pewee _____

☐ Cuban Pewee (A) _____

☐ Yellow-bellied Flycatcher _____

☐ Acadian Flycatcher _____

☐ Alder Flycatcher _____

☐ Willow Flycatcher _____

☐ Least Flycatcher _____

☐ Hammond's Flycatcher _____

☐ Gray Flycatcher _____

☐ Dusky Flycatcher _____

☐ Pacific-slope Flycatcher _____

☐ Cordilleran Flycatcher _____

☐ Buff-breasted Flycatcher _____

☐ Black Phoebe _____

☐ Eastern Phoebe _____

☐ Say's Phoebe _____

Family / Species	Date / Location Seen

❏ Vermilion Flycatcher _____

❏ Dusky-capped Flycatcher _____

❏ Ash-throated Flycatcher _____

❏ Nutting's Flycatcher (A) _____

❏ Great Crested Flycatcher _____

❏ Brown-crested Flycatcher _____

❏ La Sagra's Flycatcher _____

❏ Great Kiskadee _____

❏ Sulphur-bellied Flycatcher _____

❏ Piratic Flycatcher (A) _____

❏ Variegated Flycatcher (A) _____

❏ Tropical Kingbird _____

❏ Couch's Kingbird _____

❏ Cassin's Kingbird _____

❏ Thick-billed Kingbird _____

❏ Western Kingbird _____

❏ Eastern Kingbird _____

❏ Gray Kingbird _____

❏ Loggerhead Kingbird (A) _____

❏ Scissor-tailed Flycatcher _____

❏ Fork-tailed Flycatcher _____

❏ Rose-throated Becard _____

❏ Masked Tityra (A) _____

SHRIKES (*LANIIDAE*)

❏ Brown Shrike (A) _____

Family / Species   Date / Location Seen

❏ Loggerhead Shrike _____
❏ Northern Shrike _____

VIREOS (*VIREONIDAE*)
❏ White-eyed Vireo _____
❏ Thick-billed Vireo _____
❏ Bell's Vireo _____
❏ Black-capped Vireo _____
❏ Gray Vireo _____
❏ Yellow-throated Vireo _____
❏ Plumbeous Vireo _____
❏ Cassin's Vireo _____
❏ Blue-headed Vireo _____
❏ Hutton's Vireo _____
❏ Warbling Vireo _____
❏ Philadelphia Vireo _____
❏ Red-eyed Vireo _____
❏ Yellow-green Vireo _____
❏ Black-whiskered Vireo _____
❏ Yucatan Vireo (A) _____

CROWS AND JAYS (*CORVIDAE*)
❏ Gray Jay _____
❏ Steller's Jay _____
❏ Blue Jay _____
❏ Green Jay _____

Family / Species	Date / Location Seen

❑ Brown Jay _____
❑ Florida Scrub-Jay _____
❑ Island Scrub-Jay _____
❑ Western Scrub-Jay _____
❑ Mexican Jay _____
❑ Pinyon Jay _____
❑ Clark's Nutcracker _____
❑ Black-billed Magpie _____
❑ Yellow-billed Magpie _____
❑ Eurasian Jackdaw _____
❑ American Crow _____
❑ Northwestern Crow _____
❑ Tamaulipas Crow _____
❑ Fish Crow _____
❑ Chihuahuan Raven _____
❑ Common Raven _____

LARKS (*ALAUDIDAE*)
❑ Sky Lark (I)_____
❑ Horned Lark _____

SWALLOWS AND MARTINS (*HIRUNDINIDAE*)
❑ Purple Martin _____
❑ Cuban Martin (A)_____
❑ Gray-breasted Martin (A)_____
❑ Southern Martin (A)_____
❑ Brown-chested Martin (A)_____

Family / Species	Date / Location Seen

❏ Tree Swallow _____

❏ Violet-green Swallow _____

❏ Bahama Swallow _____

❏ Northern Rough-winged Swallow _____

❏ Bank Swallow _____

❏ Cliff Swallow _____

❏ Cave Swallow _____

❏ Barn Swallow _____

❏ Common House-Martin (A) _____

CHICKADEES AND TITMICE (*PARIDAE*)

❏ Carolina Chickadee _____

❏ Black-capped Chickadee _____

❏ Mountain Chickadee _____

❏ Mexican Chickadee _____

❏ Chestnut-backed Chickadee _____

❏ Boreal Chickadee _____

❏ Gray-headed Chickadee _____

❏ Bridled Titmouse _____

❏ Oak Titmouse _____

❏ Juniper Titmouse _____

❏ Tufted Titmouse _____

PENDULINE TITS (VERDIN) (*REMIZIDAE*)

❏ Verdin _____

Family / Species   Date / Location Seen

LONG-TAILED TITS (BUSHTIT) (*AEGITHALIDAE*)
❏   Bushtit _____

NUTHATCHES (*SITTIDAE*)
❏   Red-breasted Nuthatch _____
❏   White-breasted Nuthatch __._____
❏   Pygmy Nuthatch _____
❏   Brown-headed Nuthatch _____

CREEPERS (*CERTHIIDAE*)
❏   Brown Creeper _____

WRENS (*TROGLODYTIDAE*)
❏   Cactus Wren _____
❏   Rock Wren _____
❏   Canyon Wren _____
❏   Carolina Wren _____
❏   Bewick's Wren _____
❏   House Wren _____
❏   Winter Wren _____
❏   Sedge Wren _____
❏   Marsh Wren _____

DIPPERS (*CINCLIDAE*)
❏   American Dipper _____

BULBULS (*PYCNONOTIDAE*)

❑ Red-whiskered Bulbul (I) _____

KINGLETS (*REGULIDAE*)

❑ Golden-crowned Kinglet _____
❑ Ruby-crowned Kinglet _____

OLD WORLD WARBLERS AND GNATCATCHERS (*SYLVIIDAE*)

❑ Middendorff's Grasshopper-
    Warbler (A) _____
❑ Lanceolated Warbler (A) _____
❑ Wood Warbler (A)_____
❑ Dusky Warbler _____
   Yellow-browed Warbler (A) _____
❑ Arctic Warbler _____
❑ Blue-gray Gnatcatcher _____
❑ California Gnatcatcher _____
❑ Black-tailed Gnatcatcher _____
❑ Black-capped Gnatcatcher _____

OLD WORLD FLYCATCHERS (*MUSCICAPIDAE*)

❑ Narcissus Flycatcher (A) _____
❑ Mugimaki Flycatcher (A) _____
❑ Red-breasted Flycatcher (A)_____
❑ Siberian Flycatcher (A) _____
❑ Gray-spotted Flycatcher (A) _____

Family / Species	Date / Location Seen

❏ Asian Brown Flycatcher (A) _____

THRUSHES (*TURDIDAE*)
❏ Siberian Rubythroat (A) _____
❏ Bluethroat _____
❏ Siberian Blue Robin (A) _____
   Rufous-tailed Robin (A) _____
❏ Red-flanked Bluetail (A)_____
❏ Northern Wheatear _____
❏ Stonechat (A)_____
❏ Eastern Bluebird _____
❏ Western Bluebird _____
❏ Mountain Bluebird _____
❏ Townsend's Solitaire _____
❏ Orange-billed Nightingale-
   Thrush (A)_____
❏ Veery _____
❏ Gray-cheeked Thrush _____
❏ Bicknell's Thrush _____
❏ Swainson's Thrush _____
❏ Hermit Thrush _____
❏ Wood Thrush _____
❏ Eurasian Blackbird (A) _____
❏ Eyebrowed Thrush (A)_____
❏ Dusky Thrush (A)_____
❏ Fieldfare _____
❏ Redwing (A) _____

Family / Species   Date / Location Seen

❏   Clay-colored Robin _____
❏   White-throated Robin (A) _____
❏   Rufous-backed Robin _____
❏   American Robin _____
❏   Varied Thrush _____
❏   Aztec Thrush _____

BABBLERS (WRENTIT) (*TIMALIIDAE*)
❏   Wrentit _____

MOCKINGBIRDS AND THRASHERS (*MIMIDAE*)
❏   Gray Catbird _____
❏   Black Catbird (A) _____
❏   Northern Mockingbird _____
❏   Bahama Mockingbird _____
❏   Sage Thrasher _____
❏   Brown Thrasher _____
❏   Long-billed Thrasher _____
❏   Bendire's Thrasher _____
❏   Curve-billed Thrasher _____
❏   California Thrasher _____
❏   Crissal Thrasher _____
❏   Le Conte's Thrasher _____
❏   Blue Mockingbird (A) _____

STARLINGS AND MYNAS (*STURNIDAE*)
❏   European Starling (I) _____

Family / Species	Date / Location Seen

☐ Common Myna (I) _____
☐ Crested Myna (I) _____
Hill Myna (I) _____

ACCENTORS (*PRUNELLIDAE*)
☐ Siberian Accentor (A) _____

WAGTAILS AND PIPITS (*MOTACILLIDAE*)
☐ Yellow Wagtail _____
☐ Citrine Wagtail (A) _____
☐ Gray Wagtail (A) _____
☐ White Wagtail _____
☐ Black-backed Wagtail _____
☐ Tree Pipit (A) _____
☐ Olive-backed Pipit (A) _____
☐ Pechora Pipit (A) _____
☐ Red-throated Pipit _____
☐ American Pipit _____
☐ Sprague's Pipit _____

WAXWINGS (*BOMBYCILLIDAE*)
☐ Bohemian Waxwing _____
☐ Cedar Waxwing _____

SILKY-FLYCATCHERS (*PTILOGONATIDAE*)
☐ Gray Silky-flycatcher (A) _____
☐ Phainopepla _____

Family / Species	Date / Location Seen

OLIVE WARBLER (*PEUCEDRAMIDAE*)

☐ Olive Warbler _____

WOOD-WARBLERS (*PARULIDAE*)

Bachman's Warbler (E) _____
☐ Blue-winged Warbler _____
☐ Golden-winged Warbler _____
☐ Tennessee Warbler _____
☐ Orange-crowned Warbler _____
☐ Nashville Warbler _____
☐ Virginia's Warbler _____
☐ Colima Warbler _____
☐ Lucy's Warbler _____
☐ Crescent-chested Warbler (A) _____
☐ Northern Parula _____
☐ Tropical Parula _____
☐ Yellow Warbler _____
☐ Chestnut-sided Warbler _____
☐ Magnolia Warbler _____
☐ Cape May Warbler _____
☐ Black-throated Blue Warbler _____
☐ Yellow-rumped Warbler _____
☐ Black-throated Gray Warbler _____
☐ Golden-cheeked Warbler _____
☐ Black-throated Green Warbler _____
☐ Townsend's Warbler _____
☐ Hermit Warbler _____

Family / Species	Date / Location Seen
❏ Blackburnian Warbler	_____
❏ Yellow-throated Warbler	_____
❏ Grace's Warbler	_____
❏ Pine Warbler	_____
❏ Kirtland's Warbler	_____
❏ Prairie Warbler	_____
❏ Palm Warbler	_____
❏ Bay-breasted Warbler	_____
❏ Blackpoll Warbler	_____
❏ Cerulean Warbler	_____
❏ Black-and-white Warbler	_____
❏ American Redstart	_____
❏ Prothonotary Warbler	_____
❏ Worm-eating Warbler	_____
❏ Swainson's Warbler	_____
❏ Ovenbird	_____
❏ Northern Waterthrush	_____
❏ Louisiana Waterthrush	_____
❏ Kentucky Warbler	_____
❏ Connecticut Warbler	_____
❏ Mourning Warbler	_____
❏ MacGillivray's Warbler	_____
❏ Common Yellowthroat	_____
❏ Gray-crowned Yellowthroat	_____
❏ Hooded Warbler	_____
❏ Wilson's Warbler	_____
❏ Canada Warbler	_____

Family / Species	Date / Location Seen

❏ Red-faced Warbler _____
❏ Painted Redstart _____
❏ Slate-throated Redstart (A) _____
❏ Fan-tailed Warbler (A) _____
❏ Golden-crowned Warbler _____
❏ Rufous-capped Warbler _____
❏ Yellow-breasted Chat _____

BANANAQUIT (*COEREBIDAE*)

❏ Bananaquit _____

TANAGERS (*THRAUPIDAE*)

❏ Hepatic Tanager _____
❏ Summer Tanager _____
❏ Scarlet Tanager _____
❏ Western Tanager _____
❏ Flame-colored Tanager _____
❏ Western Spindalis _____

NEW WORLD SPARROWS (*EMBERIZIDAE*)

❏ White-collared Seedeater _____
   Cuban Grassquit (I) _____
❏ Yellow-faced Grassquit (A) _____
❏ Black-faced Grassquit (A) _____
   Red-crested Cardinal (I) _____
❏ Olive Sparrow _____
❏ Green-tailed Towhee _____

	Family / Species	Date / Location Seen
❏	Spotted Towhee	_____
❏	Eastern Towhee	_____
❏	Canyon Towhee	_____
❏	California Towhee	_____
❏	Abert's Towhee	_____
❏	Rufous-winged Sparrow	_____
❏	Cassin's Sparrow	_____
❏	Bachman's Sparrow	_____
❏	Botteri's Sparrow	_____
❏	Rufous-crowned Sparrow	_____
❏	Five-striped Sparrow	_____
❏	American Tree Sparrow	_____
❏	Chipping Sparrow	_____
❏	Clay-colored Sparrow	_____
❏	Brewer's Sparrow	_____
❏	Field Sparrow	_____
❏	Worthen's Sparrow (A)	_____
❏	Black-chinned Sparrow	_____
❏	Vesper Sparrow	_____
❏	Lark Sparrow	_____
❏	Black-throated Sparrow	_____
❏	Sage Sparrow	_____
❏	Lark Bunting	_____
❏	Savannah Sparrow	_____
❏	Grasshopper Sparrow	_____
❏	Baird's Sparrow	_____
❏	Henslow's Sparrow	_____
❏	Le Conte's Sparrow	_____

Family / Species	Date / Location Seen

❏ Nelson's Sharp-tailed Sparrow _____

❏ Saltmarsh Sharp-tailed Sparrow _____

❏ Seaside Sparrow _____

❏ Fox Sparrow _____

❏ Song Sparrow _____

❏ Lincoln's Sparrow _____

❏ Swamp Sparrow _____

❏ White-throated Sparrow _____

❏ Harris's Sparrow _____

❏ White-crowned Sparrow _____

❏ Golden-crowned Sparrow _____

❏ Dark-eyed Junco _____

❏ Yellow-eyed Junco _____

❏ McCown's Longspur _____

❏ Lapland Longspur _____

❏ Smith's Longspur _____

❏ Chestnut-collared Longspur _____

❏ Pine Bunting (A) _____

❏ Little Bunting (A)_____

❏ Rustic Bunting _____

❏ Yellow-throated Bunting (A) _____

❏ Yellow-breasted Bunting (A) _____

❏ Gray Bunting (A)_____

❏ Pallas's Bunting (A) _____

❏ Reed Bunting (A)_____

❏ Snow Bunting _____

❏ McKay's Bunting _____

CARDINALS AND ALLIES (*CARDINALIDAE*)

❏ Crimson-collared Grosbeak _____
❏ Northern Cardinal _____
❏ Pyrrhuloxia _____
❏ Yellow Grosbeak _____
❏ Rose-breasted Grosbeak _____
❏ Black-headed Grosbeak _____
❏ Blue Bunting _____
❏ Blue Grosbeak _____
❏ Lazuli Bunting _____
❏ Indigo Bunting _____
❏ Varied Bunting _____
❏ Painted Bunting _____
❏ Dickcissel _____

BLACKBIRDS, ORIOLES, AND ALLIES (*ICTERIDAE*)

❏ Bobolink _____
❏ Red-winged Blackbird _____
❏ Tricolored Blackbird _____
❏ Tawny-shouldered Blackbird (A) _____
❏ Eastern Meadowlark _____
❏ Western Meadowlark _____
❏ Yellow-headed Blackbird _____
❏ Rusty Blackbird _____
❏ Brewer's Blackbird _____
❏ Common Grackle _____
❏ Boat-tailed Grackle _____

Family / Species	Date / Location Seen

- ❑ Great-tailed Grackle _____
- ❑ Shiny Cowbird _____
- ❑ Bronzed Cowbird _____
- ❑ Brown-headed Cowbird _____
- ❑ Black-vented Oriole (A) _____
- ❑ Orchard Oriole _____
- ❑ Hooded Oriole _____
- ❑ Streak-backed Oriole _____
- ❑ Bullock's Oriole _____
- ❑ Spot-breasted Oriole (I) _____
- ❑ Altamira Oriole _____
- ❑ Audubon's Oriole _____
- ❑ Baltimore Oriole _____
- ❑ Scott's Oriole _____

FINCHES AND ALLIES (*FRINGILLIDAE*)

- ❑ Common Chaffinch (A) _____
- ❑ Brambling _____
- ❑ Gray-crowned Rosy-Finch _____
- ❑ Black Rosy-Finch _____
- ❑ Brown-capped Rosy-Finch _____
- ❑ Pine Grosbeak _____
- ❑ Common Rosefinch (A) _____
- ❑ Purple Finch _____
- ❑ Cassin's Finch _____
- ❑ House Finch _____
- ❑ Red Crossbill _____

Family / Species   Date / Location Seen

☐ White-winged Crossbill _____
☐ Common Redpoll _____
☐ Hoary Redpoll _____
☐ Eurasian Siskin (A)_____
☐ Pine Siskin _____
☐ Lesser Goldfinch _____
☐ Lawrence's Goldfinch _____
☐ American Goldfinch _____
  European Goldfinch (I) _____
☐ Oriental Greenfinch (A) _____
  Yellow-fronted Canary (I) _____
  Common Canary (I) _____
☐ Eurasian Bullfinch (A)_____
☐ Evening Grosbeak _____
☐ Hawfinch (A)_____

OLD WORLD SPARROWS (*PASSERIDAE*)
☐ House Sparrow (I)_____
☐ Eurasian Tree Sparrow (I) _____

WEAVERS (PLOCEIDAE)
☐ Orange Bishop (I) _____

ESTRILDID FINCHES (*ESTRILDIDAE*)
  Nutmeg Mannikin (I) _____
  *Java Sparrow (I)*_____

POTTER STYLE

Art courtesy of The Scott Russo Archive/artarchives.com

Species Checklist from *The Sibley Guide to Bird Life and
Behavior* by The National Audubon Society and
David Allen Sibley, copyright © 2002 by Chanticleer Press, Inc.,
published by Alfred A. Knopf, Inc. Reprinted by permission of
Alfred A. Knopf, Inc.

Design by Marysarah Quinn and Patrice Sheridan
Published by Clarkson Potter/Publishers, Random House, Inc.
www.clarksonpotter.com
Printed in China
ISBN-13: 978-0-307-33891-4
ISBN-10: 0-307-33891-6